OOPS!

TOO MUCH NOISE

AJAY BAIRAGI

Copyright © AJAY BAIRAGI
All Rights Reserved.

This book has been self-published with all reasonable efforts taken to make the material error-free by the author. No part of this book shall be used, reproduced in any manner whatsoever without written permission from the author, except in the case of brief quotations embodied in critical articles and reviews.

The Author of this book is solely responsible and liable for its content including but not limited to the views, representations, descriptions, statements, information, opinions and references ["Content"]. The Content of this book shall not constitute or be construed or deemed to reflect the opinion or expression of the Publisher or Editor. Neither the Publisher nor Editor endorse or approve the Content of this book or guarantee the reliability, accuracy or completeness of the Content published herein and do not make any representations or warranties of any kind, express or implied, including but not limited to the implied warranties of merchantability, fitness for a particular purpose. The Publisher and Editor shall not be liable whatsoever for any errors, omissions, whether such errors or omissions result from negligence, accident, or any other cause or claims for loss or damages of any kind, including without limitation, indirect or consequential loss or damage arising out of use, inability to use, or about the reliability, accuracy or sufficiency of the information contained in this book.

Made with ♥ on the Notion Press Platform
www.notionpress.com

Contents

Acknowledgements

This book is more than just words on paper — it's a reflection of the love, support, and inspiration I've been blessed with throughout my journey.

First and foremost, I dedicate *OOPS: TOO MUCH NOISE* to my beloved daughter, **Karya Ajay Bairagi**. You are my greatest joy, my guiding light, and the reason I strive to be better every day. Your laughter, curiosity, and boundless spirit inspire me to dream bigger and push harder. This book is for you, my little star — may you always chase your dreams fearlessly and stay true to your own voice.

To my incredible **family** — my loving wife and my parents — thank you for being my strong pillars of strength. Your belief in me, even when the world was filled with noise and doubt, gave me the courage to keep moving forward. Every word in this book carries a piece of your love and encouragement.

A heartfelt thank you to my amazing team at **The Business Fame Magazine**. Your dedication, creativity, and relentless passion continue to inspire me. Together, we've created something extraordinary — and I'm grateful for every step of this journey with you.

A special note of gratitude to **Riya Gote** — a phenomenal content creator, self-awareness trainer, and the brilliant author of *The Hangman's Diary: Mantras. Meanings. Manifestations.* Your wisdom, insight, and deep support have been instrumental in shaping this book. Your ability to help others find their voice and purpose is truly remarkable, and I'm honoured to have your guidance and collaboration.

To everyone who believed in me, challenged me, and stood by my side — thank you. This book exists because of you.

— Ajay Bairagi

Note To Readers

Why OOPS: TOO MUCH NOISE? Because if there's one thing I've learned in life — and I'm sure you have too — it's that the world around us is rarely silent.

The noise is everywhere.

It's in the doubts people cast on your dreams, the unsolicited opinions about your choices, the criticism that often outweighs encouragement. It's in the fear of failure and the pressure to fit into expectations that were never yours to begin with.

And sometimes, the loudest noise comes from within — the voice that questions if you're good enough, strong enough, or ready enough.

This book is about silencing that noise. It's about tuning out the distractions, the negativity, and the naysayers — and tuning in to your own vision, belief, and strength. Through Radha's journey, you'll see how staying true to your purpose and pushing forward despite the noise can lead to incredible growth and success.

I hope this book reminds you that the noise around you will never fully disappear — but you have the power to rise above it. Define yourself before the world tries to do it for you. Believe in your vision, even when no one else does.

Because when the noise fades, what remains is your voice — and that's the one that truly matters.

— Ajay Bairagi

CHAPTER I

Breaking the Silence

The sun had just begun its ascent, casting a golden hue over Pune's bustling streets. The city, a perfect blend of tradition and modernity, was already stirring.

Kothrud, once a quiet suburb, had transformed into a thriving hub of students, professionals, and entrepreneurs. The aroma of freshly brewed chai from roadside stalls mingled with the crisp morning air, while the rhythmic chants from the neighborhood temple echoed through the narrow lanes.

Amidst this morning symphony — chirping birds outside her window, the distant hum of traffic, and the rhythmic ticking of the old wall clock — Radha Joshi sat cross-legged on the cool marble floor of her one-bedroom apartment.

Her eyes were gently shut, her breath slow and measured, as her fingers moved instinctively over the smooth, timeworn beads of her healing mala. Each bead carried the weight of whispered prayers, silent hopes, and an unshaken faith that anchored her in the present.

The *Hanuman Chalisa* played softly from her phone, its familiar verses wrapping around her like a protective cocoon, shielding her from the noise of the outside world. Each syllable, each rhythmic chant, was more than just a prayer — it was a bridge between her restless mind and an unshakable inner peace.

The words, ingrained in her memory since childhood, carried the weight of faith, resilience, and a quiet strength that had seen her through life's many storms.

It wasn't just devotion; it was grounding.

A sacred thread that wove her past, present, and future into a single moment of stillness. As she sat there, absorbing the soothing cadence of the verses, she felt her breath steady, her heartbeat sync with the rhythm, her worries momentarily dissolving like mist in the morning sun.

This ritual was as essential as the first rays of light touching her skin, a gentle reminder that before she stepped into the chaos of the world — before she answered emails, faced expectations, and navigated the unspoken pressures of the day — she had to return to herself first.

In these precious moments of solitude, she wasn't defined by roles, responsibilities, or the judgments of others. She simply existed, held by the power of devotion and the quiet assurance that, no matter what the day brought, she would face it with deep strength.

In a world that constantly questioned her choices — why she wasn't married yet, why she had traded a corporate career for spiritual healing, why she chose solitude over convention — this was her rebellion wrapped in stillness. Here, on this sacred patch of marble, she was not a daughter, a friend, or a woman expected to conform. She was simply Radha, untangled from expectations, at peace with her own rhythm.

Radha, 29, was not the kind of woman people expected her to be. She didn't fit neatly into society's boxes — neither the docile, agreeable woman molded by tradition nor the fiery rebel who rejected it entirely. Instead, she carved her own space somewhere in between, unapologetically herself.

Her long, wavy black hair was usually tied in a messy bun — not as a fashion statement, but as a silent testament to her ever-busy mind, always lost in thought, always moving, always questioning.

Some strands inevitably slipped free, framing her face in a way that made her look effortlessly defiant. Her dusky skin, kissed by the sun and untouched by fairness creams, carried the warmth of her heritage, while her sharp eyes held a quiet intelligence, the kind that made people uncomfortable because they knew she saw more than she let on.

Her posture was straight, shoulders squared, as if she carried an invisible armor forged by the battles she had fought — some against the world, many within herself. She had learned to stand her ground, not with aggression, but with the quiet confidence of a woman who knew her worth.

She was neither conventionally feminine nor overtly rebellious. She didn't chase validation through delicate graces, nor did she seek attention through loud defiance. She was simply Radha — unfiltered, unrestrained, and unwilling to shrink herself to fit expectations that were never hers to begin with.

Born and raised in Pune, Radha had always felt a pull toward the road less traveled, the one that veered away from the familiar, well-trodden paths of her peers.

Growing up, she had a natural curiosity about the world around her, not content with just answering the questions, but with asking them. It was no surprise that she found herself drawn to writing and storytelling at a young age — expressing thoughts, ideas, and emotions through words gave her a sense of freedom she couldn't find elsewhere.

Her education in Business and Marketing had laid a strong foundation, providing her with the technical expertise and strategic insights that many would consider essential for success in the corporate world.

But for Radha, these skills were tools, not defining features. They gave her the means to navigate the complexities of the business landscape, but her true calling lay elsewhere — in the world of stories, ideas, and expression.

She had always known that the corporate mold wasn't for her. The idea of climbing a corporate ladder, dressed in suits and playing by unspoken rules, never quite appealed to her.

While her peers moved steadily up the ranks in their corporate jobs, collecting titles and promotions, Radha chose a different path.

She ventured into the uncharted waters of entrepreneurship, building something from the ground up — a content and magazine startup. It wasn't just about creating a business for her; it was about giving voice to stories that mattered, crafting narratives that resonated with people, and building a platform where creativity and purpose could thrive.

She poured her heart and soul into her startup, knowing that success would come not through conformity, but through authenticity and the courage to stay true to her passions.

The noise had started the moment Radha announced her decision over breakfast which was eight months ago.

That morning, the sunlight streaming softly through the kitchen window as the smell of freshly brewed chai lingered in the air. Her parents, seated at the table with her, exchanged glances — her mother's brow furrowed in concern, her father's face a mix of disbelief and worry.

"Why not take up a stable job?" her mother asked, her voice laced with a mixture of practicality and concern.

"You've worked so hard for your degree. Why throw it all away on something so uncertain? A steady job with a good salary, that's what every parent wants for their child. Why go against the tide?"

She pushed a plate of toast toward Radha, as if trying to feed her a sense of stability.

Radha sighed softly, looking out the window, letting the stillness of the morning settle in before responding. She had anticipated this conversation, but it didn't make it any easier.

"Mom, I appreciate your concern. But this is what I want to do. I've always loved writing, and I believe in this. A job can give me stability, but it can never give me purpose. This magazine, it's more than a career to me — it's a dream, and I have to chase it."

Her tone was calm, but her eyes were resolute.

Her father, who had been silently stirring his tea, finally spoke up. His voice was stern, his words sharp with skepticism.

"Who will invest in a woman-led magazine firm, Radha? This isn't the kind of business that thrives. It's a niche market. A magazine? In this day and age? You're better off doing something more practical, something that guarantees a future. You've always been so bright — don't waste it on something that might not even pay off."

Radha felt the weight of his words, but she didn't flinch.

She had heard similar doubts many times before, and each one only made her more determined.

"I know it's a risk, Dad. But what's life without risk? I'm not looking for a shortcut to success, and I'm not doing this just for money. Writing is my passion. People will read stories that matter, they'll connect with them. It's not about the short term, it's about creating something meaningful."

Her mother, shaking her head, tried once more. "But writing is just a hobby, Radha. You can write in your free time. You don't need to build an entire company around it. Think about your future. Think about security."

Radha's voice softened, but there was a fire behind it that made her parents pause. "Writing is my future, Mom. I want to create a space where my voice — and the voices of others — can be heard. It's not about security; it's about fulfilment.

I know you want what's best for me, but sometimes what's best doesn't look like what you expect. I'm ready for this. I need to do this."

The room grew silent for a moment. Her parents, still processing her words, exchanged a long glance.

Radha sat still, feeling both the weight of their concern and the weight of her own resolve. Her dream was already in motion, and no matter what, she was ready to let it unfold.

Her family, although supportive in their own way, was skeptical. They couldn't quite grasp why she would choose to walk a path that seemed uncertain, even reckless.

They loved her, and their concern came from a place of wanting her to succeed in a world that often didn't make it easy for women to thrive.

Her parents, while cautiously supportive, often offered advice that came across as more of a warning. Yet, they remained her safety net, offering her the comfort of home and the hope that maybe — just maybe

— her dreams would find their place in the world.

But it was her extended family that truly tested her resolve. Her relatives, particularly those who had long embraced conventional career paths, were vocal in their disapproval. During family gatherings, she could feel their eyes on her like a constant weight, their judgment sharp and unspoken in every glance.

"Who starts a business in magazines? It's a dying industry!" her uncle had said one evening at a wedding, his tone as dismissive as his words. "The world's moving fast — who's going to sit down and read a magazine? Why not something more practical, like a tech startup or a consultancy? Something with real potential!"

His words echoed in Radha's mind, a harsh reminder of how her dreams seemed so out of place in their world.

And as for her aunts and cousins, their disapproval often came wrapped in 'concerned' advice. "You're so talented, dear. But think about security," one aunt had whispered over cups of tea at a family gathering, her voice laced with subtle judgment.

"You can't just live on passion. Why not stick to something stable, something that won't leave you struggling?" Another cousin, with a knowing smirk, chimed in, "A magazine? And as a woman? People will question your credibility. You need a proper backup plan."

Radha could practically hear the collective hum of doubts and assumptions that circled around her. The whispers, the sideways glances, the carefully worded suggestions — all these things created a chorus of 'noise' that she had long learned to filter out.

At first, the weight of it all had been overwhelming. She would question herself, wondering if maybe they had a point. Maybe she was making a mistake. But over time, she began to realize that their opinions — though well-intentioned—weren't her truth.

Her passion for storytelling, her vision for creating a space where voices could be heard, wasn't something they could understand. They had grown up in a world that valued stability and tradition.

To them, taking a leap into something like a magazine business, especially as a woman, seemed risky, almost foolish. But Radha had learned that their fears, their judgments, weren't hers to carry. She didn't need their approval to build her dream.

At family events, where the discussions would inevitably turn to her "unconventional" choices, Radha had learned to smile politely and nod when they offered their advice.

She had learned to tune out the noise.

Her journey was hers alone, and she had made peace with the fact that some people would never understand her path. She didn't need validation from those who couldn't see the world the way she did.

She had long since realized that her success wouldn't come from convincing others; it would come from staying true to herself, even if it meant standing alone.

Two months back Radha had moved to Kothrud not just to change her surroundings but to carve out a life that was truly her own, away from the suffocating expectations that had weighed her down for years.

Pune, with its familiar streets and faces, had always felt like a place where others' expectations hung like invisible threads, pulling her in directions she didn't always want to go. She had outgrown the tight-knit neighbourhood where everyone knew her name and felt entitled to an opinion about her life.

Kothrud, with its mix of quiet residential lanes and buzzing energy from nearby cafes and co-working spaces, was a place where she could breathe freely. It wasn't just a change of address — it was a symbolic step toward freedom, a declaration that she was going to live life on her own terms.

Her apartment, though small, was a reflection of her personality — imperfectly perfect. The walls, though not lavish, were lined with books she had collected over the years, a personal library that told the story of her journey — novels, business strategy books, travel journals, and magazines that had inspired her to follow her passion.

The stacks of books weren't just decor; they were reminders of the countless hours she had spent reading, learning, and dreaming of building something of her own. Each book was a chapter of her own evolving story, filled with wisdom, experiences, and lessons that she had carefully curated.

Her desk, a simple wooden piece that had seen better days, was a chaotic landscape of sticky notes. Ideas, quotes, reminders, and half-formed thoughts were plastered all over the surface, crammed into the corners of her vision.

There were no neat piles or organized spaces—just a constant overflow of thoughts and creativity that never stopped. The sticky notes weren't just a way of staying organized; they were a visual representation of her mind, constantly moving, constantly creating. They were her mental landscape, tangible proof that she was always working, always dreaming, always building.

Above her desk hung a vision board that anchored her focus — a collection of images, words, and aspirations that encapsulated the essence of her goals.

In bold, handwritten letters were the words that defined her journey: *Clarity. Courage. Communication. Confidence.*

These were the 4C's she lived by.

They weren't just words on a board — they were the principles that guided her every decision.

Clarity in her vision, courage to follow it even when others doubted her, the power of communication to share her message, and confidence in her ability to make it happen.

Every time she looked at that board, she was reminded of why she had chosen this path and the values that would help her stay true to it, no matter the obstacles.

Her space was hers — untamed, unpolished, but brimming with purpose. It was here, in the quiet chaos of her apartment, that Radha built her dreams, piece by piece. Every corner, every object, every note on the wall was a testament to her determination to create something that was uniquely hers.

It wasn't just about building a business — it was about building a life that reflected who she truly was, free from the expectations of the world around her. And in this small, cluttered apartment, away from the noise of outside opinions, Radha had found her sanctuary.

As she finished her morning meditation, Radha took a deep breath, letting the quiet settle within her. She slowly opened her eyes, grounding herself in the stillness that enveloped her.

The morning light filtered softly through the window, casting long shadows across her apartment, the same space where so many dreams had been nurtured. In those precious moments of silence, she felt a deep connection to herself — strong, calm, and ready to face the day ahead. Today was no ordinary day; it was another battle.

She stood up, stretching her arms above her head, allowing the tension from the previous days to melt away. Her heart was racing, and her mind began to churn with thoughts of the upcoming pitch.

She had been here before — facing rejection from the same investor who had dismissed her last time. His words had stung then, leaving her with a sense of doubt she couldn't quite shake. "It's a risky venture for a woman-led company," he had said, his tone indifferent, as though it was all too predictable. "Maybe try again when you have more traction."

But if there was one thing Radha Joshi never did, it was give up. She had been knocked down more times than she could count, and each time, she rose again.

Each failure, each rejection, was simply another step in the process of proving to herself — and to the world — that she was capable. Her determination was unshakable.

Today, she was ready to walk into that meeting with the same courage that had carried her through the toughest of days.

As she walked toward her desk, the city outside roared to life — car engines revving, the hum of conversations rising, and the rhythmic thump of footsteps on the pavement. The sounds of Pune's morning hustle were a sharp contrast to the calm that radiated within her.

It was the same city that had both supported her and tested her, but today, she was not distracted by its noise. She had learned that the external chaos would never stop; it would always be there, loud and persistent, ready to drown out the quiet confidence she had fought so hard to cultivate.

Inside her apartment, though, it was different. Inside, she was centered—anchored in the quiet power of her own resolve. The noise outside would always try to disrupt her focus, but she had mastered the art of tuning it out.

It was almost like the world outside her window existed in a parallel dimension, one she could observe but not be affected by. The real noise, she realized, was inside the mind—the doubts, the questions, the insecurities. But she had learned to quiet those too, drowning them with a steady stream of her own conviction.

Radha sat down at her desk, taking a moment to breathe again. The sticky notes with ideas, the vision board with her 4C's, the scattered books — all of it was a reminder that she had already won half the battle.

She didn't need validation from others to know her worth. She knew who she was, and she knew what she was capable of.

Today, the pitch was just another step forward, a new challenge to face, but it wouldn't define her. Whether she succeeded or not, she would keep going.

The world could judge her, question her, or even reject her, but she would never stop fighting for her dream.

With a steady hand, she adjusted her laptop, readying herself for the call. The investor might still be skeptical. The noise would remain.

But Radha was ready.

And nothing, not even rejection, could stop her now.

CHAPTER II

The Weight of Words

The warmth of the sun streamed through Radha's window, but inside her heart, there was a chill. She had just returned from a family gathering, a place where the weight of judgment hung in the air like a heavy fog. The words of her relatives and well-meaning friends had burrowed deep into her thoughts, a constant echo that she couldn't shake off.

"You really think you can build a business in the magazine industry? In this economy?" her cousin Priya had said with a scoff, her voice laced with doubt. "What experience do you have? Writing is just a hobby, Radha. Not a career."

Radha had forced a smile and nodded politely, but inside, her mind was spinning. The judgment felt like a stone pressing against her chest, heavy and suffocating. She tried to explain her vision, her dreams, but their skepticism only seemed to grow.

"You should've gone for a stable job. That's the only way to make it. This entrepreneurial thing—it's risky, especially for a woman," her uncle had chimed in, shaking his head. "You can't always rely on passion. Sometimes, practicality has to take the lead."

The voices followed her all the way home, their criticism reverberating in her mind.

As she sat down at her desk, she could still hear their words, as if they were written on the walls of her small apartment. She knew they meant well, in their own way, but their doubt felt like a boulder being thrown into her path.

Radha closed her eyes, the weight of the day pressing down on her shoulders. The noise of her family's voices still echoed in her mind, but she knew she had to quiet them, if only for a moment.

Taking a deep breath, she allowed the air to fill her lungs, holding it for a moment before slowly releasing it.

With each exhale, she felt the tension in her body slowly dissolve. The quiet of her apartment, the steady rhythm of her breath, and the stillness she had created were her sanctuary, a space she had built with purpose. It was here, in this calm, that she could reconnect with herself and the vision that had driven her from the beginning.

In this space, there were no doubts. No judgments. No voices telling her what she should be doing. This was the place where Radha was allowed to be unapologetically herself.

She reminded herself that the opinions of others, though well-intentioned, were just that — opinions.

They were shaped by their own experiences, their own fears, and their own limitations. But they were not facts. They didn't define her.

"They want what's best for me," Radha thought, but that didn't mean they understood the path she was walking. Her journey was uniquely hers, and only she knew the reasons behind every choice she made. Their doubts were born out of their own fears, fears that didn't align with her own aspirations.

"I don't have to carry their doubts," she reminded herself.

She felt the familiar tug of insecurity at the back of her mind. What if they're right? What if I am making a mistake? What if I fail?

But Radha gently pushed these thoughts aside.

She had walked this path before — faced moments of doubt, of questioning, of fear — and each time, she had made it through. The external noise was just that — noise. It didn't have the power to derail her unless she allowed it.

Her mind wandered to the early days of her journey — the moments when she had first set out on this path. Back then, the doubts had been louder.

Every failure, every rejection felt personal. But now, she had learned to distance herself from the judgment of others. She had learned that the only voice that truly mattered was her own.

And in this moment, as she sat on her chair, surrounded by the quiet of her own thoughts, she knew deep down that this was where she belonged.

"Their opinions don't need to be my truth," she thought, finding clarity in the simplicity of the words. What her relatives and friends didn't understand — what they couldn't understand — was that her vision, her dream, wasn't meant to fit into their world.

It was hers, unique and unfolding, and she was the one who had to believe in it the most. It wasn't about their approval. It was about her deep belief in herself and in the purpose behind her venture.

Radha opened her eyes, feeling a sense of peace settle over her. The noise from the outside world hadn't stopped, but inside, she had created a space where their doubts could no longer take root.

She knew there would be more moments like this—more voices questioning her, more people who didn't see her vision, and more challenges along the way.

But in this quiet moment, she had grounded herself in something far more powerful than any external judgment: her own deep belief in what she was capable of achieving. And with that belief, she knew she could move forward, no matter what anyone else said.

But the weight of their words — of their judgment — lingered.

It wasn't just their voices she had to contend with; it was the internal dialogue that had been brewing in her mind. What if they're right? What if I'm just wasting my time? What if I fail?

She shook her head, trying to banish the thoughts. She couldn't afford to let them take root. She had to stay focused.

She had to remember her purpose.

She reached for her vision board, her eyes scanning the words she had written: *Clarity. Courage. Communication. Confidence.*

Radha let the word sink deep into her mind, repeating it to herself like a mantra.

She had spent so much of her life questioning her decisions, second-guessing herself, and seeking validation from others.

But now, as she sat alone in her apartment, surrounded by books, sticky notes, and the quiet hum of the world outside, she understood that clarity didn't come from others' approval or from external markers of success. It came from within—something that couldn't be shaken by the opinions of well-meaning relatives or disapproving friends.

She leaned back in her chair, closing her eyes once again, and let her thoughts drift to the reasons she had chosen this path. Why had she decided to leave behind a stable job and take on the immense challenge of starting her own business?

The answer was simple.

She loved stories.

The way words could bring people together, make them laugh, make them cry, make them think. That was her true calling, her passion.

And magazines were the perfect medium to share those stories. Her vision had always been to create something different — something that celebrated the richness of diverse perspectives. In a world where mainstream media often presented a one-dimensional view of success, she wanted to offer a platform where varied voices—underrepresented, unique, and bold—could be heard.

This wasn't a decision born out of following a trend or trying to fit into an established mold. Radha had always known that she didn't belong in the conventional corporate world. She wasn't interested in climbing the corporate ladder or playing by someone else's rules. She wasn't doing this to please anyone or to prove anything.

This was her own journey, and she was building something that reflected her — her values, her aspirations, and her unshakable belief in the power of storytelling.

Her mind wandered to the moments when she first began formulating this idea. She had always been an avid reader, fascinated by how magazines could capture the pulse of society, how they could influence culture and create change.

She remembered the countless nights spent reading articles, flipping through pages, and imagining herself in the editorial chair, shaping stories that mattered. But more than that, she remembered the way certain stories had made her feel — a sense of connection, understanding, and empathy. It was this feeling that had driven her to start her own venture.

The more she thought about it, the clearer it became. This was not a passing idea, a fleeting dream. It was something deeper. Something lasting. Radha wasn't simply building a magazine company.

She was creating a space for herself—a platform for her voice to be heard, and for the voices of others who had been overlooked.

And even though many of her friends, family, and mentors couldn't see her vision yet, she understood that it didn't matter. They couldn't see the future as she could. They couldn't understand the fire that burned inside her every time she thought about the stories she wanted to tell. But she did. Her clarity came from her passion, her purpose, and the knowledge that this was the right path for her.

As she sat back and reflected on this, Radha felt a sense of calm wash over her. The noise, the doubts, the criticisms — they were all just static. They didn't change her vision. They didn't change her purpose.

Her dream was clear. She was building something for herself. And that was enough.

Courage. Radha reflected on the word, letting it resonate deeply within her. It wasn't some grand, dramatic act of bravery that she was after. It wasn't about waiting until all the fear disappeared, or until she had everything figured out.

No, courage, she had come to understand, wasn't the absence of fear. It was the ability to move forward despite it — the willingness to keep going, even when every part of her wanted to stop.

She remembered the early days, when the thought of leaving her stable job seemed like an insurmountable mountain. The fear of the unknown had gripped her, cold and suffocating.

The voices of doubt — both from within and from the people around her—had made it even harder to take the first step.

"What if it all falls apart? What if I fail?" The questions had been endless.

But somehow, even with all the fear swirling inside her, Radha had found the courage to walk away. She had always known that following her passion would come with risks, with sacrifices.

But what scared her more than the fear of failure was the idea of living a life that wasn't hers. A life spent following a path that others had laid out for her, a life where she'd never get to pursue the things that truly set her heart on fire.

That fear, the fear of regret, had pushed her forward.

And even when she took that leap—leaving behind a secure job, the comfort of a pay check, and the expectations of others—she hadn't been free of fear. It hadn't magically disappeared.

In fact, it only grew louder. The constant questions about her decision, the raised eyebrows from friends and family, the whispers behind her back — every single one of them had been a reminder that fear was still there, lurking, reminding her of the risks she was taking.

But Radha had learned something valuable: Fear was inevitable. It was part of the process.

The real courage, she realized, was in embracing the fear and continuing to move forward anyway.

Every rejection, every setback had become part of her journey, not a sign of failure, but an opportunity to learn and grow. She remembered the many times she had faced rejection — be it from potential clients, investors, or even people she'd hoped would support her.

Each "no" had stung, but with every rejection, Radha had learned to stand taller.

"It's not a defeat," she would tell herself after each failure. "It's a lesson."

And she'd kept that mantra close to her heart, using every failure as fuel for her determination. The "no's" had become stepping stones, leading her toward the "yes" that would eventually come. She had learned that rejection wasn't a reflection of her worth or her ability; it was simply a part of the process.

Each time she felt the sting of rejection, she reminded herself that it wasn't the end. It was one more opportunity to refine her approach, one more chance to sharpen her skills, one more lesson to learn.

And with each rejection, she had grown more resilient. More steadfast.

She had learned that courage wasn't just about the big moments of decision—it was in the daily commitment to push forward, even when the road felt uncertain.

And so, despite the fear of failure that would always linger in the background, Radha kept moving. She kept fighting. She kept believing. Because deep down, she knew that every step forward, no matter how small, was a step closer to the breakthrough she was waiting for.

Her journey wasn't easy, and the fear would never completely go away. But as long as she kept moving forward, she knew she was living with courage — one step at a time.

Communication. For Radha, this wasn't just a skill — it was the very essence of who she was. She had always been a writer at heart, someone who found solace and strength in the written word. Words were her power, her weapon, and her gift.

As a child, she had always gravitated toward stories — whether in books, magazines, or the stories she wrote herself. It was through writing that she first discovered her voice, and it was through writing that she learned how to connect with others.

Her love for communication ran deep. She knew that stories could change the world — one well-crafted sentence, one meaningful paragraph at a time.

Whether it was an article, a personal reflection, or even a pitch to an investor, Radha had always believed that the ability to communicate her thoughts, ideas, and vision clearly was her superpower. The challenge, she realized, wasn't in the act of convincing others—it was in making them see what she saw.

She had a vision for her magazine. She could picture the stories, the voices, the message, the impact it would have on the world.

But her challenge was in translating that vision into words—words that could make others feel the same passion, excitement, and purpose that she felt. It wasn't just about selling an idea; it was about conveying the why behind it—the deeper purpose, the soul of the business that made it different from everything else out there.

The most difficult part, however, was staying true to her voice. Radha had learned early on that in the world of business, especially as a woman starting her own company, there was constant pressure to conform. To speak in ways that felt safe, to mold her ideas to fit into what others wanted to hear.

There were times when her confidence wavered, when she questioned whether her voice was too raw, too unpolished, too different from what the world expected. But every time she felt this way, she reminded herself that authenticity was key. She had to communicate in her own voice, not in the voice of those around her.

The pressure to fit in was real. Her investors, her mentors, and even her friends sometimes suggested that she modify her approach, tone down her ideas, make her language more "professional" or "mainstream."

But Radha knew that if she started compromising on her voice—if she started filtering out the parts of her that made her unique—she would lose the very essence of what made her business special. She would lose the spark that had ignited her vision in the first place.

So, Radha committed herself to communicating in her own way. She leaned into her authenticity, refusing to let the noise of external opinions drown out her true voice.

Whether it was in the pitch meetings with investors, in the articles she wrote, or in the conversations she had with her team, she made sure to communicate her passion, her vision, and her values in the most genuine way possible.

It wasn't always easy, especially when others seemed to question her every move, but she knew that staying true to her voice would be what set her apart.

In her writing, she poured herself out — she used it as a tool to express her thoughts, to challenge the status quo, and to spark new ideas.

Each word she wrote was a piece of her soul laid bare, and she had learned that the more vulnerable and authentic she was in her communication, the more it resonated with others.

The struggle, however, was not always about the words themselves — it was about the confidence to speak them aloud. Radha knew that communication wasn't just about putting thoughts into sentences; it was about believing in those words and being willing to stand behind them. Even when others didn't understand, even when they doubted her vision, she had to remain steadfast and clear in her communication.

Her biggest challenge now was to ensure that the vision she had for her magazine — the unique, bold, and unapologetic voice she wanted to amplify — was communicated in every aspect of the business.

It wasn't enough to just create great content; she had to convey the spirit of that content through every interaction, every marketing strategy, and every pitch to investors.

As she stared at the blank page on her screen, Radha reminded herself that words were not just tools for communication — they were also tools for change. Her magazine could challenge societal norms, amplify unheard voices, and tell the stories that mattered.

And to do that, she had to stay true to the words she used, not just for herself but for everyone who believed in her vision.

She had learned that her communication, if done authentically and powerfully, could move people, inspire them, and ultimately make them see the world as she did. And that was the ultimate power.

Confidence. For Radha, this was the hardest one of all. She had spent years battling the inner voices that questioned her worth, her capabilities, and her decisions.

Even as she built her business, there were moments when self-doubt crept in like a silent storm, threatening to destabilize the foundation she had worked so hard to create. She often found herself wondering if she was truly capable of leading a magazine firm, especially when the world around her seemed to question her every move.

The criticisms, the unsolicited advice, and the well-meaning doubts from family, friends, and mentors had a way of seeping into her consciousness, making her second-guess herself. It wasn't easy to block out the noise, and there were times when she felt like an imposter in her own business.

But over time, Radha had come to realize that confidence wasn't about being perfect or flawless — it was about trusting herself, her ideas, and the journey she had chosen.

She had learned that confidence wasn't something that came overnight. It wasn't about waking up one day and suddenly feeling invincible; it was a practice, an ongoing commitment to believe in herself even when others couldn't see her vision.

Confidence was something she had to actively cultivate every day, through every challenge and setback.

The fear of failure was always lurking just beneath the surface. There were moments when Radha felt paralyzed by the thought of failing — of pouring so much of herself into something only to have it fall apart.

But with time, she came to understand that failure wasn't the end.

It wasn't a reflection of her abilities or her worth. Failure, she learned, was simply another lesson in disguise — a stepping stone on the path to success.

She had failed before.

She had pitched her idea to investors who laughed it off, telling her that starting a magazine in today's digital age was a fool's errand. She had faced rejections from clients who didn't believe in her vision.

She had encountered moments of burnout where she wondered if she was in over her head.

Yet, with each failure, she had come back stronger. The setbacks didn't define her—they refined her. They taught her resilience and perseverance. Every time she stumbled, she picked herself up, dusted herself off, and kept moving forward.

Confidence wasn't about avoiding failure — it was about learning to embrace it as part of the journey.

Radha had also learned that confidence wasn't just about trusting her abilities—it was about trusting the process. She knew that building a business, especially one as personal and unique as hers, wasn't going to be a smooth ride.

There would be bumps, twists, and turns along the way. But what mattered was her belief in the vision she had created and in her ability to adapt, pivot, and grow.

It wasn't always easy.

There were days when she felt overwhelmed by the weight of expectations—her own and others'. There were times when she questioned if she had what it took to lead, to innovate, and to overcome the hurdles in her path.

But in those moments of doubt, she reminded herself that confidence wasn't about having all the answers. It was about having the courage to take the next step, even when the path ahead wasn't clear.

Radha's confidence was built on a foundation of self-trust. She trusted that she had the wisdom to navigate through challenges, that she could learn from her mistakes, and that she could adjust her approach when necessary.

Her confidence was rooted in the belief that she was enough — not because she was flawless or without fear, but because she was willing to show up every day, do the work, and keep evolving.

She didn't need to be perfect; she needed to be authentic. Radha's journey wasn't about creating a flawless business or being the perfect entrepreneur — it was about owning her story, accepting her imperfections, and finding the strength to move forward despite her fears.

In those moments when she felt vulnerable or uncertain, she reminded herself that her authenticity was her greatest asset. The world didn't need a perfect leader — it needed a leader who was real, who was willing to grow, learn, and adapt.

As Radha stood before the mirror that morning, ready to face another day of challenges, she repeated her mantra quietly to herself: *"I trust myself. I trust my vision. I trust my journey."*

Confidence, she knew, wasn't just about having all the answers—it was about embracing the uncertainty, the risks, and the unknown with faith in her own abilities. It was about knowing that the road would be tough, but that she was tougher.

She wasn't perfect, and she didn't need to be. What mattered was that she believed in herself, and that belief, Radha knew, would carry her through every challenge, every setback, and every fear.

Confidence was a muscle, and she was determined to make it stronger with every step she took forward.

She closed her eyes again, focusing on the 4C's.

These weren't just words on a board. They were the pillars of her life, the foundation on which she would build her business, her identity, and her future.

She had learned to filter out the noise from her relatives, her friends, and even the well-meaning mentors who offered unsolicited advice. Their voices didn't define her. They were merely background noise in the grand symphony of her life.

As the day wore on, Radha sat at her desk, reflecting on the morning's conversations. She wrote in her journal, letting the ink flow freely, capturing her thoughts and fears. "Their words won't be my truth unless I let them.

Their doubts won't define my journey unless I allow them to. I choose my own path, even if it's difficult. I choose to rise above their judgments and prove to myself what I'm capable of."

She finished writing, a sense of calm washing over her. The weight of her relatives' words had lessened, replaced by a sense of inner strength.

She could hear their voices, yes, but now they were fading into the background, drowned out by her own clarity, courage, communication, and confidence.

Radha stood up from her desk, a newfound sense of determination filling her.

She wasn't just building a business — she was building herself. Each challenge, each setback, was an opportunity to strengthen her resolve. The world might judge her, question her, or dismiss her, but Radha Joshi knew one thing for certain: she would never stop.

CHAPTER III

Building a Tribe

Radha's office was not the glass-and-steel high-rise one would expect from a rising entrepreneur. Instead, it was a cozy, vibrant space on the second floor of an old commercial building in Kothrud, Pune. Large windows let in the morning sun, casting a warm glow on the wooden desks cluttered with books, magazines, and coffee mugs with motivational quotes.

A massive whiteboard hung on one wall, filled with ideas, deadlines, and random doodles — a mix of creativity and chaos. Right in the center was a framed poster with the words, *The Bold Type – A Magazine for the Fearless.*

This was Radha Joshi's vision come to life. A magazine startup that wasn't just about writing but about telling stories that mattered.

And now, it was time to build the right team to take it forward.

Radha leaned against the doorway of her office, arms crossed, watching as Pratik Naik stepped inside. He scanned the space like a detective arriving at a crime scene—calculating, skeptical, already questioning his life choices.

"You look like you're about to regret this decision," Radha teased, a smirk playing on her lips.

Pratik let out a dry chuckle. "I do regret this decision. A magazine startup? In 2024? You do know print is practically on life support, right?"

Radha shrugged, unfazed. "Good thing we're not just a magazine, then. We're building a brand, a movement, a storytelling revolution."

Pratik raised an eyebrow. "A revolution, huh? And how exactly do you plan to make money with this 'revolution'?"

She grinned. "By being smarter than everyone who thinks it's impossible."

Pratik exhaled, shaking his head. "Great. I walked into a cult."

Radha laughed. "No, you walked into The Narrative. And if you play your cards right, you might just help build something legendary."

He studied her for a moment. He wasn't fully convinced, but damn—her confidence was something else. "Fine. But if this turns into a disaster, I'm reserving my right to say 'I told you so'."

Radha winked. "Deal. But you won't get the chance."

Radha spotted Raghav Deshmukh lingering awkwardly near the entrance, shifting from foot to foot like he wasn't sure if he should be here. His messy curls, oversized backpack, and slightly panicked expression made him look like a college student who had wandered into the wrong building.

"You lost, kid?" Radha called out, leaning on her desk with an amused smile.

Raghav straightened up instantly. "Uh—no! I mean, I think... I work here now?" He adjusted his backpack as if it contained the answer to all his doubts.

Radha chuckled. "You think you work here? That's not very reassuring."

Raghav gulped. "No, I mean—I do! Definitely. It's just... I've never worked in a real office before."

She raised an eyebrow. "You do know this isn't exactly a 'real' office, right? No cubicles, no HR breathing down your neck, and definitely no one expecting you to have all the answers."

He let out a nervous laugh. "Yeah, that actually makes it worse. What if I mess up?"

Radha walked over and clapped a hand on his shoulder. "Then you mess up. Big deal. The only way to fail here is by not trying. Just show up, learn, and stop overthinking."

Raghav exhaled. "Okay... I can do that."

Radha grinned. "Good. Welcome to The Bold Type, Raghav. Now, drop the 'Am I good enough?' act. You wouldn't be here if you weren't."

For the first time that day, Raghav smiled. Maybe—just maybe—he belonged here after all.

Radha looked up from her laptop just as Pooja Yadav walked in, balancing a cup of chai in one hand and a neatly organized planner in the other. Her crisp cotton saree—always perfectly pleated—gave her an air of quiet authority, and her short, effortlessly styled hair only added to the impression that she had life completely figured out.

"You know, Pooja," Radha smirked, "every time you walk in, I feel like I need to get my life together."

Pooja raised an eyebrow, setting her chai down on the desk. "You do need to get your life together, Radha. You can't run a business on caffeine and last-minute ideas."

Radha gasped dramatically. "Excuse me! My ideas are brilliant."

Pooja sighed, flipping open her planner. "Brilliant, yes. Structured? No. That's where I come in." She tapped her pen on the table. "Speaking of which, our deadlines don't care about your 'creative process.' We need the next edition of The Bold Type ready for print by Friday."

Radha groaned. "Ugh. Deadlines. My least favorite thing."

Pooja sipped her chai, unbothered. "Mine too. But you know what I like more than deadlines?"

Radha squinted at her. "What?"

"Getting paid." Pooja smiled sweetly. "And for that, we need an actual schedule. Now, stop sulking and show me what you've got so far."

Radha chuckled, shaking her head. "Fine, fine. But just so you know, you're officially the responsible adult in this company."

Pooja smirked. "Good. Someone has to be."

And with that, she pulled out a stack of neatly arranged documents, ready to turn Radha's chaos into something brilliant—on schedule, of course.

Radha stood in the middle of the office, hands on her hips, surveying her new team. This is it, she thought. They had talent, they had drive, but they also had baggage.

The first few weeks were... rough.

Pratik questioned everything. Raghav second-guessed himself at every turn. And Pooja—well, Pooja just gave them all disapproving looks while somehow keeping the entire operation afloat.

But beneath her no-nonsense demeanor, Pooja was more than just a taskmaster. She was a mentor, one who knew how to shape raw potential into something remarkable. And that was why she had joined The Bold Type—not just for the challenge but because she saw something rare in Radha.

One evening, as deadlines loomed and tension ran high, Radha found herself pacing the office. "Alright, team. We're messy, we're chaotic, and honestly, we're kind of a disaster." She grinned. "But I've seen worse. And guess what? They made it work."

Pooja raised an eyebrow. "You do realize we are the 'they' you're talking about, right?"

Radha laughed. "Exactly. And that means we figure it out. Together."

For the first time that day, Raghav looked less nervous. Pratik smirked. And Pooja? She simply shook her head with an amused sigh.

They weren't perfect. Far from it. But with the right guidance, trust, and maybe just a little bit of structured chaos, they would become something unstoppable.

"Raghav, I need the draft by noon."

"Uh...yeah...so, about that..."

Pooja sighed, pinching the bridge of her nose. "Raghav, a deadline is a deadline."

Pratik leaned back in his chair, smirking. "Kid, if you don't learn to meet deadlines now, you'll be eaten alive in this field."

"I'm trying, okay?" Raghav muttered, shifting awkwardly. He wanted to prove himself, but every small mistake made him feel like he didn't belong.

And then there was Pratik.

"This pitch is weak," he told Radha after reviewing her investor presentation. "We need numbers, projections, a strong hook. Right now, it's just idealism."

Radha clenched her jaw. "It's vision. Investors don't just fund numbers, Pratik. They fund passion."

"Investors fund what makes money," he countered.

It wasn't hostility; it was friction. They all wanted the same thing—success. But trust? That had to be built.

One evening, as the team gathered for a late-night brainstorming session, Radha stood up and wrote on the whiteboard:

Clarity. Courage. Communication. Confidence.

She turned to them. "These aren't just words. This is how we survive."

Pratik raised an eyebrow. "We're running a business, Radha. Not a self-help seminar."

She grinned. "Maybe. But tell me, what's your biggest fear?"

He hesitated. "Failure."

"Exactly. And what do we do about it?"

He sighed. "We keep going."

"That is courage," she said.

Then she turned to Raghav. "You struggle to speak up in meetings. But your ideas are great. That's a communication issue, not a talent issue."

Raghav blinked. "I—I guess..."

"Confidence will come," Pooja added. "When you learn to trust yourself."

Radha nodded. "And clarity? That's knowing why we're doing this in the first place."

For the first time, the noise quieted. They weren't just colleagues. They were a team.

And together, they were going to build something extraordinary.

Radha leaned against her desk, looking at her team—each of them carrying their own battles, their own noise. She knew that success wasn't just about strategy; it was about people.

"Listen," she said, her voice steady yet warm, "I didn't start The Narrative to play it safe. We're here to build something real—something bold. Doubt, criticism, setbacks—they will never stop. But neither will we. We don't let the noise define us. We set the tone. We write our own story."

She met their eyes one by one, letting her conviction sink in. "So let's do what we do best — turn every challenge into a chapter worth reading."

A determined silence followed, then a nod from Pratik, a small but confident smile from Raghav, and a look of deep trust from Pooja.

The team was ready — not because the path was easy, but because they had Radha leading the way.

CHAPTER IV

The Investor's Dilemma

32

Radha leaned against her desk, arms crossed, watching as Pooja scrolled through her tablet.

"So, Palash Dixit," she began, "seasoned investor, serial entrepreneur, and professional skeptic. The guy has the poker face of a seasoned gambler and the patience of a bomb squad technician."

Pooja looked up, intrigued. "And he's interested in The Bold Type? That's a surprise."

"Interested is a strong word. He's...watching," Radha corrected. "He doesn't invest in just businesses; he invests in people. And according to him, I'm an unproven bet."

Pooja smirked. "I take it he told you that directly?"

Radha rolled her eyes. "Oh, in the most charming way possible. 'Startups run on vision, but survive on grit. I don't see the grit yet.' His exact words."

"So what's the game plan?" Pooja asked, closing her tablet.

"Show him the grit," Radha replied with a determined grin. "We have a pitch meeting with him in two days. We need to convince him that The Bold Type is more than just a passion project — it's a business with longevity."

Palash Dixit arrived precisely on time.

Dressed in a crisp navy blue suit, with salt-and-pepper hair and an air of effortless authority, he had the look of a man who had seen a hundred startups rise and fall. His expression was unreadable as he took a seat in the conference room.

Radha exhaled, stealing a quick glance at her team. Pratik, ever the marketer, sat poised, ready to counter any objections.

Raghav was nervously adjusting his notebook, and Pooja? Pooja was cool as ever, arms folded, observing Palash like a chess player sizing up her opponent.

"Alright, Radha," Palash said, steepling his fingers. "Convince me. Why The Bold Type? Why now?"

Radha smiled, exuding a confidence that masked the slight tremor of nerves in her chest. "Because storytelling isn't dying—it's evolving. Because people crave narratives that resonate with them. The Bold Type isn't just a magazine; it's a movement. It's a platform for voices that matter."

Palash nodded but remained impassive. "Passion is great, Radha, but passion doesn't pay the bills. Where's the revenue? Where's the market edge?"

Pratik jumped in, laying out the monetization strategy — subscriptions, partnerships, digital campaigns. He spoke with precision, anticipating Palash's skepticism. Radha followed up with projected growth charts, brand positioning, and industry trends. But Palash's expression didn't shift.

Finally, after an intense half-hour, Palash leaned back in his chair. "You present well, Radha. But here's my concern—you're too idealistic. The media industry is ruthless. What happens when the numbers don't align with the vision?"

Radha didn't hesitate. "Then we adapt. We pivot. We fight." She met his gaze head-on. "I know what you see when you look at me—a young woman trying to make it in a cutthroat industry.

But let me tell you something, Mr. Dixit—I've built this company from nothing, without connections or deep pockets. I've fought skepticism, rejections, and setbacks. And I'm still standing.

The Bold Type isn't just an idea; it's inevitable. With or without your investment, we're going to make it work. The only question is — do you want in?"

Silence hung in the room.

Palash studied her for a long moment. Then, unexpectedly, he chuckled. "Now that's grit," he said, standing up. "I'll think about it."

As he left, Radha released the breath she had been holding. Pratik gave her an approving nod, while Raghav whispered, "I think you just scared the hell out of him."

Pooja smirked. "Good. Maybe now he'll take us seriously."

The meeting had ended, but the real test had just begun. Would Palash invest? Radha didn't know. But one thing was certain—she had left an impression. And sometimes, that was the first step to winning the game.

The Storm Within

The office of The Bold Type had an undeniable buzz of energy, but beneath the surface, cracks were forming. Doubt, that insidious whisper, had found its way into the minds of even the strongest among them.

Raghav sat at his desk, staring at a blank document. His messy curls fell over his forehead as he anxiously tapped his pen against the table. The words just wouldn't come.

"What if I'm not good enough?" he thought. "What if I mess up and everyone finds out I don't belong here?"

Imposter syndrome was Raghav's constant companion.

It whispered in his ear every time he opened his laptop, making him second-guess his skills, his intelligence, and even his right to be part of The Bold Type.

Fresh out of college, surrounded by professionals who spoke with authority and executed ideas with precision, he felt like a child pretending to be an adult. He had no groundbreaking achievements, no impressive portfolio—just raw enthusiasm and a degree in Mass Communication that suddenly felt inadequate.

Every meeting felt like a test he was failing. When he pitched ideas, his voice wavered, and he braced himself for someone to call him out: You don't belong here.

The pressure to prove himself weighed him down, making even the simplest tasks feel monumental. Writing a social media post took hours, not because he lacked skill but because he feared judgment. He overanalysed every word, convinced that he would be exposed as a fraud.

But Radha had noticed his struggle.

One afternoon, after watching him delete yet another draft, she leaned against his desk and asked, "Do you know how I started?"

Raghav blinked up at her. "By being a genius?"

She snorted. "By writing horrible articles no one wanted to publish. I overthought everything, just like you. I'd rewrite the same sentence ten times, convinced it wasn't good enough. The only difference between me then and me now is that I kept writing."

Raghav swallowed. "But what if I'm just... not good enough?"

Radha's expression softened. "No one feels 'good enough' when they start. Not me, not Pooja, not even Pratik. The trick isn't to be perfect, Raghav. It's to keep showing up, even when you doubt yourself. Especially when you doubt yourself."

That conversation became his anchor.

Over time, Raghav developed a habit to silence the imposter voice—he set a timer and forced himself to write without stopping. No overthinking, no editing, just writing. He called it his 15-minute chaos draft. It wasn't perfect, but it got him started.

And slowly, something changed.

The fear didn't disappear, but it lost its grip. He started speaking up more in meetings, pitching ideas with a little more confidence. He still had moments of doubt, but now, he had a counter-voice—Radha's words echoing in his mind.

You don't have to be perfect. You just have to start.

And so, he did.

Raghav knew that talent wasn't enough — discipline had to take over where confidence failed. Slowly, he built a super habit — structured consistency.

He realized that his biggest hurdle wasn't skill but hesitation. So, he created a system that removed the need for motivation: just show up and do the work.

He dedicated the first hour of his day solely to writing. No distractions, no second-guessing. Even if he felt uninspired, even if his mind whispered that he wasn't good enough, he sat down and wrote. The goal wasn't perfection — it was progress.

At first, his inner critic screamed louder than ever. He cringed at his drafts, feeling they were amateurish, but he pushed through. He adopted a two-step process.

Write without judgment – He allowed himself to be messy, to make mistakes, to produce work that wasn't great.

Refine later – He gave himself permission to edit only after a cooling-off period, removing the pressure of perfection in the moment.

He believed in - Tracking Progress, Not Perfection.

To keep himself accountable, Raghav created a progress journal. Every day, he jotted down what he had worked on — not how good it was, but simply that he had done it. Over time, this visual proof of consistency became stronger than his doubts.

Weeks passed. The doubts didn't vanish overnight, but something changed. The more he wrote, the more natural it became. His confidence stopped being tied to his emotions and started being built on evidence of his own effort.

And then, one day, he realized something. He no longer needed motivation to start. He no longer questioned whether he belonged.

He had trained his mind to focus on doing the work, not proving his worth.

Structured consistency had done what talent alone never could—it made Raghav unstoppable. But he wasn't the only one fighting internal battles.

Across the office, Pratik paced near the window, arms crossed. Unlike Raghav, his struggle wasn't about proving himself as a newcomer. He had been here before—he had pitched, negotiated, and convinced investors before. He knew the game inside out.

But expertise doesn't silence self-doubt. It just raises the stakes.

Raghav's structured consistency had been about building skill through discipline, but Pratik's struggle was different — his was about overcoming the ghosts of failure. He had done everything right in the past and still seen things fall apart.

Now, as he stared at Palash Dixit's business card on his desk, a familiar voice echoed in his mind: What if this is another failure? What if you're not as good as you think?

Both Raghav and Pratik had different battles, yet the core challenge was the same — learning to trust themselves.

For Raghav, trust came from action. The more he wrote, the less his doubts mattered.

For Pratik, trust had to come from reframing failure — from realizing that experience wasn't just about wins but also about how he had survived the losses.

Doubt thrives in uncertainty, but action kills hesitation.

As Pratik took a deep breath and sat down to refine the pitch strategy, he wasn't just preparing numbers. He was reminding himself that he had done this before — and he could do it again.

"Remember what happened last time? You backed a failing project. You lost investors' trust. What if it happens again?"

Pratik had seen businesses collapse under bad leadership before, and he couldn't shake the fear that history would repeat itself.

The memories still clung to him — late nights in boardrooms where desperate founders made reckless decisions, partners who had promised the world but failed to deliver, and investors who had once been allies turning into adversaries when the numbers didn't add up.

One particular failure haunted him the most. Years ago, he had been part of a promising startup in the digital marketing space.

The company had everything — an innovative product, strong early traction, and a talented team. But leadership had been its downfall. The founder, obsessed with rapid scaling, ignored warnings about financial sustainability.

Pratik had spoken up, cautioned them about unsustainable spending, but he had been dismissed as overly cautious.

Within months, the company crumbled under its own weight, leaving employees stranded and investors furious.

It wasn't just the loss of the company that stung — it was the realization that he hadn't been able to prevent it.

Now, as he looked at The Bold Type, that fear resurfaced. He believed in Radha's vision, in the team's talent, but what if they were making the same mistakes? What if he was about to watch another dream implode, powerless to stop it?

That fear could have paralyzed him. It could have made him hesitant, second-guessing every decision. But Pratik had learned a powerful lesson: failure was only final if he didn't learn from it.

His super habit? Reframing the past.

Instead of dwelling on what had gone wrong, he started journaling lessons learned from his past experiences.

Each morning, before diving into work, he would sit down with his notebook and write -

What went wrong in past ventures?

What were the warning signs?

How could those mistakes have been prevented?

It wasn't about avoiding failure altogether — he knew that was impossible. It was about recognizing patterns, seeing the red flags before they turned into disasters.

Slowly, the fear that history would repeat itself began to fade. He wasn't the same person he had been back then. He was sharper, more experienced. And most importantly, he wasn't alone this time — The Bold Type was built on collaboration, not ego.

By reframing his past, Pratik transformed his fear into foresight. Instead of bracing for failure, he prepared for success — not by ignoring the risks but by learning how to navigate them. He realized that fear was a double-edged sword; it could paralyze him, or it could sharpen his instincts. He chose the latter.

His morning journaling sessions became a blueprint for decision-making. Instead of letting past failures haunt him, he dissected them, extracting valuable insights.

He identified the mistakes that had led to previous downfalls — unchecked ambition, lack of contingency plans, poor financial management — and turned them into guiding principles.

Whenever a challenge arose at The Bold Type, he didn't panic.

He asked himself, "Have I seen this before? What did I learn from it?" He analyzed every deal, every partnership, every expansion plan with a clear mind, balancing optimism with calculated risk.

And when doubts crept in—when the voice in his head whispered, What if this fails, too?—he had an answer ready:

"If it does, I'll know how to pivot. I'll know how to rebuild. Because I've been here before, and this time, I'm prepared."

This shift in mindset didn't just help him — it strengthened the entire team. His confidence became contagious.

When Radha worried about funding, Pratik reassured her with data-backed strategies. When Raghav battled imposter syndrome, Pratik reminded him that every expert was once a beginner.

Even Pooja, usually unshakable, found herself leaning on Pratik's ability to see solutions where others saw obstacles.

Fear no longer controlled him. Instead, it became his greatest asset. Because while others flinched at the thought of failure, Pratik had already faced it, learned from it, and come out stronger. Now, he wasn't just hoping for success—he was engineering it.

Every setback became a case study, every mistake a stepping stone. And when self-doubt crept in, he reminded himself: "I am not my past failures. I am my future successes."

If there was one person who kept The Bold Type grounded, it was Pooja. But even she wasn't immune to the weight of uncertainty. Sitting in her neatly arranged workspace, she reviewed financial projections for the tenth time that day. The numbers were tight. Too tight.

"What if we run out of money? What if this whole thing collapses?"

Unlike Raghav and Pratik, Pooja didn't fear failure — she feared inefficiency. She had seen what happened when organizations lacked discipline, and she wasn't about to let The Bold Type become one of them.

Her super habit? Radical prioritization.

She listed out every crisis they could face and created contingency plans. When fear knocked, she had answers ready. When doubts loomed, she focused on execution. Her belief? Action silences anxiety.

For Radha, the storm was both external and internal. Investors doubted her, competitors whispered that she was too young, too ambitious, too naive. The industry wasn't kind to visionaries who didn't have deep pockets.

And then, there was the worst voice of all—the one inside her own head.

"What if Palash is right? What if I don't have the grit? What if I'm just pretending?"

Radha had spent years defying expectations, but this moment felt different. Bigger. Heavier. The weight of leading an entire team, of carrying their hopes and fears along with her own, pressed on her chest.

Her super habit? Daily visualization.

Every morning, before stepping into the office, she stood in front of the mirror and pictured herself succeeding. Not in an abstract, motivational-quote kind of way—but in vivid, detailed imagery.

She imagined standing in a packed conference hall, announcing The Bold Type's expansion.

She visualized shaking hands with major investors. She felt the future before it arrived.

And slowly, belief replaced doubt.

Doubt didn't leave. The world didn't suddenly become supportive. In fact, as The Bold Type started gaining traction, the voices of discouragement grew louder. Competitors dismissed them. Industry veterans scoffed. "They won't last a year," some said. "She doesn't have the experience," others added.

But here's the thing about visionaries — they don't wait for validation. They create it.

Raghav kept writing. Pratik kept strategizing. Pooja kept structuring. Radha kept leading.

And little by little, the storm within began to quiet. Not because they had silenced the doubt, but because they had learned to work through it.

And that? That was their biggest strength.

CHAPTER VI

The Breaking Point

Radha stared at the email, her fingers gripping the edge of her desk. The words blurred together, but their impact was undeniable.

We regret to inform you that we're pulling out of the contract.

A major client. Gone.

The news spread like wildfire. Whispers in the industry turned into murmurs, murmurs into laughter.

"I knew it."

"They were overconfident."

"A startup like theirs? Bound to crash."

People who had once applauded their hustle now watched from the sidelines, waiting for The Bold Type to crumble.

Radha's phone buzzed with fake sympathy — messages laced with the kind of politeness that barely masked satisfaction.

"Hey, just heard. Tough luck. Let me know if you need anything."

"Things like this happen in business. Maybe it's time to rethink your model?"

"Honestly, you were juggling too much. Might be a blessing in disguise."

The words didn't sting. The intent behind them did.

She looked around the office. If her team had seen the messages, they didn't show it.

Pratik leaned back in his chair, scrolling through LinkedIn with an unreadable expression.

"Funny how people show their true colors when they think you're losing."

Raghav didn't even look up from his laptop. "Let them talk."

Pooja smirked, crossing her arms. "They're waiting for us to care. Let's not."

Radha exhaled slowly.

They didn't care.

Not because they were immune to failure, but because they weren't giving anyone the satisfaction of seeing them flinch.

Instead, they got back to work.

Her mind raced through the consequences. A significant chunk of The Bold Type's revenue had just disappeared. Investors would ask questions. Bills would pile up. Salaries would be delayed. The startup she had fought so hard to build now stood on the edge of collapse.

For the first time, Radha wondered if the critics were right. Startups run on vision, but survive on grit. Palash Dixit's words echoed in her mind. Had she mistaken passion for sustainability?

Across the room, Pratik slammed his laptop shut. "This is bad."

Raghav was pacing. "We have three months, max, before this snowballs into something we can't fix."

Pooja, usually the calmest among them, had gone silent.

For the first time, doubt seeped into the room like a thick fog, suffocating the confidence they had fought to build.

That night, the office was silent, except for the faint hum of Radha's laptop. The glow from the screen cast soft shadows on her face — exhausted, but determined. The team had gone home, but she couldn't. Not yet.

Beside her, a book lay open — *The Hanuman's Diary: Mantras. Meanings. Manifestations.* by Riya Gote. She had been reading it for weeks, drawn to its message of resilience and faith.

"Mantras. Meanings. Manifestations. If you know the meaning of a mantra, you can manifest the desire 10X."

Radha had always believed in hard work, in strategy, in persistence. But tonight, as she ran her fingers over the book's pages, she realized she had overlooked something just as powerful — belief.

She turned to the section on *Bajrang Baan*, a fierce invocation of Hanuman's strength, meant to remove obstacles with unshakable force. The words hit differently now.

"In times of doubt, don't look at the obstacle. Look at your power."

She exhaled, her grip tightening around the book.

The obstacle was clear — the lost client, the industry whispers, the people waiting for them to fail.

But what about her power?

Radha closed her eyes, the weight of the day pressing on her shoulders. Then, instead of drowning in fear, she let the mantra settle in her mind.

If she could manifest this dream from nothing, she could rebuild anything.

She reached for her notebook and started writing — ideas, solutions, contingency plans.

The crisis wasn't the end. It was a test. And she refused to fail.

Radha exhaled. We are not done. Not yet.

She reached for her notepad, writing down three things:

Find the opportunity within the crisis. Was there a new client they had overlooked? A pivot they hadn't considered?

Strengthen the core team. Were they aligned, or was fear clouding their judgment?

Reignite the vision. If they had lost their way, they needed to remember why they started.

The next morning, Radha called a meeting.

"We have two options," she said, looking at each of them. "We panic and let this define us, or we fight back."

Pratik leaned forward. "What's the plan?"

Radha smiled. That's loyalty. He wasn't walking away; he was looking for solutions.

Raghav, still battling his imposter syndrome, squared his shoulders. "Tell me what to do."

Pooja closed her laptop. "We don't have time to feel sorry for ourselves. Let's fix this."

They weren't breaking. They were forging.

As the meeting ended, Radha glanced at *The Hanuman's Diary: Mantras. Meanings. Manifestations.* again.

"Your faith in yourself is the only mantra you truly need."

She closed the book and stood up. Time to manifest a comeback.

CHAPTER VII

Silence the Noise, Amplify the Vision

The setback had shaken them, but it hadn't broken them.

Radha stood in the center of the conference room, her hands pressed against the table, scanning the faces of her team.

The room was heavy with silence, the kind that follows disappointment. Pratik's jaw was clenched, his frustration barely contained. Pooja was fidgeting with her pen, her usually calm demeanor cracked with worry.

Raghav avoided eye contact altogether, his eyes fixed on the notepad in front of him. They had worked too hard to come this far, only to watch it slip away.

And Radha could feel it — the fear creeping in, the doubts taking root again.

But she couldn't let it happen. Not now. Not when they were so close. Taking a steadying breath, Radha reminded herself why they had started this journey in the first place. She thought of the endless nights, the sacrifices, the vision that had kept them going.

The noise was louder than ever — the criticism, the failures, the self-doubt — but she knew that if they gave in now, they'd never make it out. They needed clarity. They needed courage. And more than anything, they needed belief.

She straightened up and spoke, her voice steady and strong. "I know you're scared. I know this feels like a setback we might not recover from.

But we didn't come this far just to come this far. Every challenge we've faced has prepared us for this moment. We silence the noise by remembering why we started — by holding on to our vision, even when everything else tells us to let go. So let's stop focusing on what's going wrong and start building what we know can go right. We've got this — together."

Radha took a deep breath, letting the weight of the moment settle before she spoke. "This isn't the first time we've been counted out.

And it won't be the last." Her words hung in the air, steady and certain.

She looked around the room, meeting each pair of anxious eyes. The doubt was familiar — she had faced it from the very beginning. Every time someone told her she was too young, too inexperienced, too ambitious, the noise had grown louder. But here they were — standing despite every prediction of failure.

And that was proof enough that they were stronger than the setbacks they faced.

She continued, her voice calm but powerful. "We've been here before — when we struggled to get our first client, when the funding seemed like a distant dream, when we questioned if we even had what it takes. And every time, we pushed through. Not because the noise stopped, but because we chose to rise above it. This moment is no different. The voices of doubt will always be there — but they don't define us. Our vision does. Our work does. And our belief in each other does."

Radha's eyes softened as she looked at her team — the people who had stood by her through every high and low.

"I know it's hard. I know you're tired. But this — this is where we prove ourselves again. Not to the world, but to us. We didn't come this far to give up when things get tough. We came this far because we believe in what we're building. And as long as we keep that belief alive, there's no noise loud enough to drown us out."

Radha's eyes landed on the whiteboard, where the words "Focus on what we can control" stood out in bold, black letters. That simple statement held a world of meaning.

It was a reminder of everything they had faced and everything they had overcome. The noise — the doubts, the criticism, the fear — had always been there. But they had no power over those voices. What they did have power over was their own effort, their own creativity, and their own resilience. And that was what had brought them this far.

She turned back to her team, her voice steady. "We can't control the setbacks. We can't control what people say about us or the obstacles that come our way. But what we can control is how we respond. We can choose to let fear paralyze us, or we can choose to stand up, regroup, and move forward. Our energy is too precious to waste on things beyond our influence. Let's pour it into the solutions we can create."

The room grew quieter, the tension slowly giving way to a sense of purpose. Radha could see the shift happening — Pratik's jaw relaxed, Pooja's fingers stilled, and Raghav finally looked up.

The reminder was clear: their strength lay in their focus.

The world outside would always have noise, but as long as they kept their eyes on what they could control — their vision, their work, their belief — they would always find a way forward.

The world outside their office walls had become a chorus of speculation and judgment. Competitors, always eager for an opportunity to pounce, were already celebrating their perceived downfall.

Rumours spread like wildfire — whispers of their instability, their inability to recover, their supposed lack of leadership.

Every setback was exaggerated, every challenge turned into a headline. It wasn't just professional rivalry; it was a feeding frenzy on their struggle, and the noise grew louder with every passing day.

Even former clients, once loyal and enthusiastic, began to waver. Doubts crept into their conversations — "Maybe they grew too fast," "Perhaps their vision was too ambitious," "What if they can't bounce back this time?"

The trust they had built was now hanging by a thread, and Radha could feel the weight of those second thoughts pressing down on her team's morale.

It was one thing to face external criticism, but the fear of losing the faith of those who had believed in them cut deeper than any competitor's taunt.

And then there were the well-meaning voices — friends and family who thought they were being practical. "Maybe it's time to consider a backup plan," they said gently. "Have you thought about taking up a more stable job?"

The words were wrapped in concern but laced with doubt. Every suggestion of a safer route felt like an echo of the noise Radha had been fighting against from the start.

But she knew one thing for sure: giving up on their vision would only prove the noise right — and that was something she refused to do.

The noise was deafening. It wasn't just the words — it was the weight of expectations, the sting of doubt, and the constant hum of fear disguised as advice. It was in the sideways glances, the subtle hesitation in a client's voice, the questions that never quite needed to be asked but hung in the air anyway.

The noise was everywhere — in their inboxes, their meetings, their own restless thoughts at night. It threatened to drown out everything they had worked so hard to build.

Radha knew her team felt it just as much as she did.

She could see it in the way Pratik's usual confidence had started to slip, his once-bold ideas now softened by caution. Pooja, the calmest among them, was more reserved than ever, measuring every word. And Raghav... Raghav was barely speaking at all, his creativity stifled by the fear of making the wrong move.

The noise was seeping into their bones, making them question their every decision — and Radha knew they couldn't survive that way.

"We have two choices," Radha continued, her voice steady but fierce, cutting through the tension like a blade. "We can let their words define us, or we can define ourselves."

The weight of that statement hung in the air. It wasn't just a choice — it was a challenge. A dare to rise above the noise and reclaim their narrative. She took a step forward, her eyes sweeping across the room, meeting each person's gaze. There was no room for doubt in her stance, no hesitation in her tone. This was the moment where they decided what kind of team they were going to be — one that crumbled under pressure or one that thrived despite it.

She let the silence stretch for a moment, giving them time to absorb the truth in her words. "We didn't come this far just to prove them right," she said, her voice softening but losing none of its strength.

"We didn't fight through every setback, every sleepless night, just to fold when things got tough. We've poured our hearts into this vision — sacrificed, struggled, and stood by each other when everything seemed to be falling apart. So tell me — are we going to let their noise become our story, or are we going to write our own?"

The room fell silent, but this time it wasn't fear that kept them quiet — it was determination. The shift was almost palpable. Pratik's jaw relaxed as his eyes sharpened with resolve.

Pooja sat a little straighter, her pen stilling in her hand. And Raghav, who had been avoiding her gaze all along, finally looked up — and in his eyes, Radha saw the spark she'd been waiting for. It was the moment when doubt turned to defiance, when uncertainty transformed into courage. And in that shared silence, they made their decision — together.

Pratik leaned back in his chair, his arms crossed and his face a mix of frustration and caution.

"Easier said than done," he muttered, his voice carrying the weight of every setback they'd faced. The room tensed again, the fear creeping back in — because he wasn't wrong. The noise outside was loud, relentless, and exhausting. It was far easier to let doubt take over than to keep believing when the odds seemed stacked against them.

Radha didn't flinch. Instead, she smiled — not out of arrogance, but because she understood that fear intimately. She'd felt it too, on the nights when she wondered if they'd make it through, when every rejection felt like a nail in their vision's coffin. "Not really," she said, her voice calm but sure.

"We silence the noise by amplifying the vision." Her words hung in the air like a challenge, simple but powerful.

She stepped away from the table and toward the whiteboard, her eyes flicking to the statement still scrawled there: Focus on what we can control.

"The noise only gets loud when we stop listening to our own voice," she continued.

"Our vision — that's our voice. It's the reason we started this journey. It's the belief that kept us going when no one else believed in us. And the louder we make that vision, the quieter their doubts become."

The room was still, but Radha could feel the shift — the slow but steady rise of hope and conviction.

Radha grabbed the marker with the kind of quiet confidence that made everyone sit up a little straighter.

She walked to the whiteboard and, with deliberate focus, underlined the words already written there: Focus on what we can control. The sound of the marker against the board was the only noise in the room — a sharp contrast to the chaos swirling outside their walls. She turned back to face her team, her eyes bright with conviction.

"We started this because we believed in something bigger than ourselves," she said, her voice steady and clear.

"That belief hasn't changed. The vision we built, the purpose we committed to — it's still here, and it's stronger than ever. The setbacks, the doubts, the noise — those are just distractions. They only have power if we let them. But our vision? That's ours. No one gets to take that away."

She looked around the room, her gaze landing on each member of the team.

"We didn't come this far because things were easy. We made it here because we dared to dream bigger, work harder, and push through when the world told us to quit. And I promise you this — if we stay focused on why we started, if we keep building on the foundation of that belief, there's no noise loud enough to drown us out."

The room was quiet, but it was a different kind of silence now. It was the kind of stillness that comes before momentum — the calm before a collective surge of determination. And in that moment, Radha knew they were ready.

Radha let the question hang in the air, her eyes moving slowly from one face to the next. She wasn't looking for blame — she was looking for reflection. The silence stretched long enough to feel heavy, but she didn't rush to fill it. She wanted them to think. To own both their mistakes and their growth.

Finally, Raghav broke the quiet. His voice was soft but steady. "We relied too much on one big client," he said, his brow furrowed in thought. "When they pulled back, we didn't have a safety net. We need to diversify — spread our risk so one loss doesn't threaten everything we've built."

Radha nodded, her expression encouraging.

"Exactly. And it's not just about finances — it's about stability, strategy, and vision. We put so much energy into keeping one client happy that we didn't leave ourselves room to grow elsewhere. That's a mistake we won't repeat."

Pratik leaned forward, his fingers tapping against the table. "We also got comfortable," he added. "We stopped pushing as hard as we did in the beginning. Maybe we took our success for granted."

Radha smiled, not in reprimand but in recognition. "That's the kind of honesty we need. The lessons aren't in the wins — they're in the setbacks. And we're going to use every one of them to come back stronger."

Pratik nodded, his mind already turning over possibilities. "And we need a more aggressive outreach strategy," he said, his voice firm.

"We've been waiting for clients to find us — that has to change. We need to show them why they need us, not the other way around." His eyes sparkled with a newfound determination. "We should be in their inboxes, on their feeds, and in their minds — consistently and confidently."

Before Radha could respond, Pooja, who had been quietly listening, finally spoke up. She straightened her shoulders and leaned forward, her calm but authoritative presence drawing everyone's attention.

"We should also rethink our pricing models," she suggested thoughtfully.

"Let's create flexible packages so startups and smaller businesses can afford us without long-term commitment. Right now, we're focused on big retainers — but there's a whole market out there that just needs a foot in the door. Let's be that door."

Radha's eyes lit up with pride. This was the team she believed in — bold, strategic, and solution-focused.

"Exactly," she said, her voice rising with energy. "We don't just react — we innovate. Let's take these ideas and turn them into action. Because the best way to silence the noise? Results. Let's make sure our success speaks so loudly, no one can ignore it."

The room shifted then — the fear and frustration replaced by a quiet, burning resolve. They weren't just weathering the storm anymore. They were preparing to rise above it.

Radha smiled. "Now we're thinking."

For the next hour, the team dove deep into their failure—not with despair, but with purpose. Every misstep was laid out on the table, not as a source of blame but as data—valuable lessons that held the key to their next breakthrough.

They analyzed the over-reliance on a single client, the gaps in their outreach, and the rigidity of their pricing models.

Radha guided the discussion with the calm assurance of a leader who knew that setbacks were just stepping stones. "We're not here to dwell on what went wrong," she said, her voice steady. "We're here to figure out how to make sure it never happens again."

As they dissected each issue, the energy in the room shifted from frustration to focus. Pratik sketched out a dynamic outreach plan, targeting multiple industries and diversifying their client base.

Raghav proposed a content strategy that would position them as thought leaders, drawing clients in through value-driven storytelling.

Pooja refined their pricing structures, introducing tiered packages that made their services accessible without compromising profitability. Every suggestion was met with collaboration, every problem with a solution. The noise outside their walls faded, drowned out by the sound of creativity and strategy taking shape.

By the time the meeting wrapped up, the room felt different. The weight of their recent setback still lingered, but it no longer felt like an anchor—it was a catalyst.

The doubt hadn't vanished entirely, but something far more powerful had taken its place: determination. It was visible in Pratik's steady gaze, in Raghav's newfound confidence, and in the quiet conviction of Pooja's smile.

They weren't just a team recovering from failure—they were a team ready to rise stronger than ever.

As they gathered their notes and prepared to get to work, Radha watched them with a quiet sense of pride. This wasn't just about survival anymore. It was about proving—to themselves and to the world—that their vision was worth fighting for. The noise would always be there. But from this point on, their focus would be louder.

As they walked out, Radha turned back and glanced at the board one last time.

Radha's eyes lingered on the words she'd underlined on the whiteboard. Simple, yet powerful — a reminder of everything they needed to hold on to when the world around them felt chaotic. The external noise — the doubts, the criticism, the unsolicited advice — was beyond their reach. But their response? Their strategy? Their resilience? That was entirely in their hands.

"We can't control the market," Radha began, her voice steady.

"We can't control what people say about us. But we can control how we show up every day — how we push forward, how we innovate, and how we refuse to let fear dictate our decisions."

The team listened, and slowly, the tension began to ease. They realized that the power to shape their future wasn't in the hands of their competitors or their critics — it was theirs. Pratik started scribbling down ideas for a new outreach strategy, his earlier frustration giving way to focus. Raghav's mind raced with creative concepts, no longer clouded by fear of failure. Pooja's calm presence became even more rooted as she thought about strengthening their internal processes.

The shift was happening — the team was evolving from a state of reaction to one of action.

They weren't just surviving.

They were evolving.

With every discussion, they were building something more resilient, more agile — a company prepared to withstand storms and seize opportunities. Their setbacks had taught them valuable lessons, and now those lessons were shaping their growth. The doubts hadn't disappeared, but they no longer controlled the narrative.

What mattered was their belief in their vision and their ability to keep moving forward, one focused step at a time.

Radha smiled as she watched the transformation unfold. This was what leadership looked like — not the absence of fear, but the courage to act in spite of it.

And as the noise outside continued to hum, it was clear that their focus, their determination, and their vision were far louder.

CHAPTER VIII

The Sweet Sound of Success

The air in the office felt different—lighter, charged with excitement and a quiet sense of accomplishment. It was a stark contrast to the heavy atmosphere that had once hung over them, thick with doubt and uncertainty.

After months of setbacks, late nights, and moments of near-collapse, Radha Joshi's startup was finally thriving.

The transformation was almost palpable.

Desks that had been cluttered with worry and desperation were now organized and brimming with purpose and energy.

Smiles were easier, conversations more hopeful, and every corner of the office buzzed with a renewed sense of optimism.

But this change hadn't come easily. The 'noise'—those relentless voices of criticism, fear, and self-doubt—had been deafening at times. It wasn't just the external noise from skeptical investors and doubtful family members questioning Radha's capabilities.

It was also the internal noise—the nagging whispers of insecurity and the echoes of past failures that threatened to drown their vision.

Every day had felt like a battle, not just against market challenges but against the cacophony of opinions and fears that tried to shake their confidence.

That noise had reached its peak during their most trying moments—when a major client backed out, when funds ran dangerously low, when even the most dedicated team members wondered if they were on a sinking ship.

The pressure was immense, the distractions constant.

And yet, Radha had stood firm. Radha's strength came from a philosophy she had embraced from her mentor, Riya, the author of *The Hanuman's Diary: Mantras. Meanings. Manifestations.* Riya had taught her the 4C's principle — *Clarity, Courage, Communication, and Confidence* — and it became Radha's guiding light.

In the face of overwhelming noise, it was these four pillars that kept her anchored and pushed her team to tune out the distractions and focus on their goals.

Clarity. Radha knew exactly why she had started this journey. The vision of building a content and branding firm that stood for creativity, authenticity, and trust was crystal clear in her mind. When doubts crept in, it was this clarity that kept her from wavering. She made sure her team understood their mission too, aligning every project and decision with their core purpose.

Courage. It took immense bravery to stand against societal norms and pursue an unconventional career. But Radha's courage went beyond starting the business—it was in every tough decision she made, every risk she took, and every time she stood up for her team. Even when a major client backed out or an investor walked away, she faced those setbacks with resilience, never letting fear dictate her choices.

Communication. In times of chaos, Radha's ability to communicate openly and honestly became their strongest tool. She kept the team informed, addressed their concerns, and ensured that everyone's voice was heard. By fostering a culture of transparency, she created a space where trust could flourish and misunderstandings could be resolved before they turned into noise.

Confidence. Perhaps the most difficult yet vital of the 4C's, confidence was the foundation on which Radha built everything. She believed in her vision when no one else did. She believed in her team's potential even when they doubted themselves. And through her deep self-assurance, she inspired those around her to believe too.

It was these principles that transformed the office from a place of anxiety to one of purpose and positivity.

The noise hadn't disappeared entirely—it never truly does.

But it had been drowned out by something far stronger: the collective belief in their vision and the courage to keep moving forward.

Now, that noise was finally fading. In its place was a quiet hum of productivity and passion. Clients were coming in, not just because of their services but because they believed in the vision Radha and her team had so fiercely protected. Investors who once doubted her leadership were now eager to be part of their success.

And perhaps most importantly, every member of the team had grown—personally and professionally—finding their own voices amidst the silence they had fought so hard to create.

It started slowly—one breakthrough client who believed in their creativity, then another. Palash Dixit, the once-skeptical investor, not only signed the deal but became one of their strongest advocates.

"You proved me wrong, Radha," he had said after their latest quarterly report showed exponential growth. "And I've never been happier to admit it."

The growth wasn't just financial—it was deeply transformative.

Pratik Naik had found his stride as the Marketing and Business Development head, evolving from a man burdened by his past failures into a leader who inspired confidence. Once hesitant and overly cautious, Pratik now made decisions with clarity and conviction, balancing strategy with intuition. He had learned from Radha's example — the importance of filtering out the noise of fear and external doubt — and channelled that lesson into his leadership. His ability to mentor others with patience and empathy made him an invaluable pillar of the company, someone his team turned to for guidance and reassurance.

Raghav Deshmukh's transformation was equally remarkable.

The once hesitant intern, unsure of his place and abilities, had blossomed into a key contributor whose ideas sparked creativity and innovation.

Through Radha's constant belief in his potential and Pratik's patient mentorship, Raghav found his voice. The self-doubt that had once shadowed his every suggestion was replaced by a quiet confidence, allowing his unique perspectives to shape some of the company's most successful campaigns.

Each time his ideas were implemented and celebrated, it reinforced his belief in his own capabilities, pushing him to take bolder steps.

Pooja Yadav remained the team's steadying force — their rock. With years of corporate experience behind her, she knew how easily a company's culture could be compromised when driven solely by ambition.

But under Radha's leadership, she helped nurture an environment of trust, collaboration, and integrity. Her wisdom often provided the balance between urgency and patience, innovation and tradition. Through moments of crisis and celebration alike, Pooja's calm, composed presence reassured the team, making her the glue that held them together.

Together, they had grown not just as professionals but as individuals. Each had faced their own form of 'noise'—Pratik's fear of failure, Raghav's imposter syndrome, and Pooja's concern for ethical stability—and emerged stronger because of it. Their collective journey of self-discovery and resilience mirrored the very foundation Radha had built the company on: a belief in one's vision, the courage to pursue it, and the strength to rise above the noise.

This personal evolution was the company's true success story, far beyond the numbers on a balance sheet.

But the real transformation was Radha's own. Success hadn't changed her—it had affirmed her. She had learned that proving herself right mattered far more than silencing her critics. The very people who once questioned her choices were now seeking her advice, but their approval no longer defined her.

One evening, as the team celebrated a record-breaking quarter, Radha stepped onto the office balcony. The city lights stretched out before her—a reminder of how far they had come. Pratik joined her, raising his glass.

"You did it, Radha," he said, his voice filled with pride.

"We did it," she corrected with a smile.

The sweet sound of success wasn't the applause or the numbers—it was the quiet satisfaction of knowing they had stayed true to their vision.

And as Radha looked back at her team, laughing and dreaming about the future, she knew their journey was just beginning.

Radha stood in front of her team, her eyes filled with pride and gratitude. "Self-confidence is your superpower," she began, her voice steady and warm. "Pratik, you've shown us exactly what that looks like. You transformed your self-doubt into strength, and now you lead with conviction and grace.

You believed in yourself when it mattered most — and that belief didn't just shape your own growth; it uplifted everyone around you. That's the power of self-confidence, and you wear it so well."

She turned toward Raghav with a gentle smile.

"Raghav, never forget your roots. I remember the day you joined us — quiet, unsure, but full of potential. And look at you now — a powerhouse of ideas and creativity. You stayed humble through your growth, and that humility kept you grounded even as your confidence soared. Your journey reminds us that knowing where we come from keeps us true to who we are."

Then, her gaze softened as it met Pooja's. "Pooja, you've taught us the importance of making the most of every moment. Through every challenge, you brought calm and wisdom. You balanced urgency with patience, ambition with ethics — and in doing so, you created a work culture where everyone feels supported and valued. Your ability to stay present and focused made all the difference."

Happy tear in eyes, Radha addressed them all. "Don't be afraid of failure. Every setback we faced taught us something invaluable. Taking a stand for yourself, your vision, and your beliefs is never easy — but it's necessary. Remember, this is your life. The noise will never stop, but it's up to you to decide which voices you listen to. Trust yourself, stay true to your values, and never stop believing in your own power. Because when you do that — as each of you has shown — success becomes inevitable."

Radha looked around the room, her voice calm but filled with conviction. "True confidence isn't about walking into a room thinking you're better than anyone else — it's about knowing you have nothing to prove. Each of you brings something invaluable to this team. Pratik, your sharp strategy. Raghav, your fresh creativity. Pooja, your steady wisdom. We didn't succeed by competing with each other — we succeeded by owning our strengths and standing together."

She smiled warmly.

"Carry your confidence like it's your armour — no one can take it from you unless you let them. Remember the days when doubt and criticism tried to shake us? We stood firm because we believed in our vision. That belief is your greatest power. Don't ever let anyone dim your light."

Her eyes softened as she continued. "The moment you believe you deserve a seat at the table, the world takes notice. I've seen this transformation in each of you. When you stopped questioning your worth and started embracing your potential, everything around you shifted — opportunities found you because you finally believed you were ready for them."

Radha's voice grew stronger, filled with passion. "Life's too short to stay in the shadows — step into the spotlight, take risks, and own your space. Every setback we faced became the foundation for our comeback. Every rejection pushed us closer to the right opportunity. Keep chasing your dreams like you were born to achieve them — because you were."

She paused, her words hanging in the air. "Your greatest strength lies in being your authentic self. Never shrink to fit someone else's idea of who you should be. Take up space, speak your truth, and embrace your uniqueness. The world doesn't need more copies — it needs your one-of-a-kind brilliance."

Radha took a deep breath, looking around at the people who had been part of this incredible journey. "When we started this company, there was so much noise — the doubts, the criticism, the constant questioning of whether we'd make it. Everyone had an opinion on what we should or shouldn't do. But here we are, not because the noise stopped, but because we stopped listening to it. We learned to tune out everything that didn't align with our vision and focus on what truly mattered — our belief in ourselves and each other."

She smiled, her eyes filled with pride and gratitude. "The noise will never completely go away. There will always be voices telling you that you're not good enough, not ready, not capable. But if there's one thing I want you to take away from this journey, it's this — the only voice that truly matters is the one inside you. Trust it. Nurture it. Let it guide you. That's how you silence the noise."

As she looked at her team — her tribe — Radha felt a quiet sense of fulfillment. "Oops: Too Much Noise — that's what they called our dream. But we turned that noise into music. We turned every doubt into determination and every failure into a lesson. And today, we stand here not because we proved them wrong, but because we proved ourselves right. This is just the beginning — let's keep making some noise, the kind that changes the world."

Epilogue

As the dust settled and the noise slowly faded, Radha stood on the balcony of her office, looking out at the city that had once seemed so overwhelming. The journey hadn't been easy — there were battles fought, doubts overcome, and sacrifices made. But through it all, one truth remained: the noise never really goes away.

You just learn how to rise above it.

Radha's success wasn't just about building a thriving startup. It was about building people — including herself. Pratik, once unsure and hesitant, had become a visionary leader. Raghav had found his voice and his confidence. Pooja's steady hand had kept them grounded and focused. And Radha? She had learned that true strength lies not in silencing others but in amplifying your own purpose.

The noise will always be there — from competitors, critics, and even your own fears. But when you stay true to your vision, when you believe in your mission, that noise becomes background static. What takes center stage is your passion, your resilience, and the story you choose to write.

As Radha walked back inside, the office was buzzing — not with fear or doubt, but with energy, creativity, and purpose. And in that moment, she knew: they weren't just surviving anymore. They were thriving.

Because when you focus on what truly matters, the noise doesn't stand a chance.

About The Author - Ajay Bairagi

When you think of visionaries shaking up the media and advertising industry, Ajay Bairagi's name is bound to pop up.

With over seven years of hands-on experience, Ajay has been on a mission — not just to lead, but to revolutionize. He's the mastermind behind innovative solutions that bridge the gap between leaders and organizations, creating powerful platforms where entrepreneurs don't just dream — they showcase, shine, and thrive.

An engineering graduate with an MBA in marketing, Ajay has always believed that connecting people and building dynamic teams are the ultimate superpowers in business. And trust me, he wields those powers like a pro.

As the Director of The Business Fame, he helms a squad of creative geniuses, delivering groundbreaking business solutions to leaders across the globe.

But it's not all smooth sailing — and that's where Ajay's true grit shines through. His journey has been a masterclass in resilience and adaptability.

Every challenge faced has been a stepping stone, every setback a setup for a comeback. He's not just about surviving the storm — he's about dancing in the rain and coming out stronger, bolder, and smarter.

What keeps him ahead of the curve? An insatiable curiosity and an unrelenting drive to learn. Ajay believes the world's evolving at lightning speed — and staying curious, adaptable, and open to new experiences is the secret sauce to thriving in any industry.

Oh, and did we mention the accolades? This man's trophy shelf is stacked. From the Business Excellence Award and National Icon Award to the World Signature Award and Corporate Titan Award, Ajay's been celebrated far and wide for his leadership and vision.

But he's not just a man of titles — he's a man of impact. As the founder and director of The Business Fame and co-founder of Business Iconic, Metapreneur, The Education Fame, and City Cars, Ajay's influence stretches across industries. He's the force behind powerhouse events like Globex Business Conclave & Awards, Indian Leadership Summit & Awards, and the Maharashtra Udyog Gaurav Awards, to name just a few.

In short? Ajay Bairagi isn't just making noise — he's making history. And trust us, this is just the beginning.

www.ingramcontent.com/pod-product-compliance
Lightning Source LLC
Chambersburg PA
CBHW040131150726
48005CB00015B/2450